WITH TEARS IN OUR EYES

Richard E. Lauersdorf

Northwestern Publishing House
Milwaukee, Wisconsin

To all those
with whom I have shared
earth's sorrow and heaven's victory
at the death of a loved one

Second printing,   2004

Cover art by Gary Crabbe/Enlightened Images

Northwestern Publishing House
1250 N. 113th St., Milwaukee, WI 53226-3284
© 2003 by Northwestern Publishing House
www.nph.net
Published 2003
Printed in the United States of America
ISBN 0-8100-1557-9

Contents

1

WITH TEARS IN OUR EYES

"Woman," he said, "why are you crying? Who is it you are looking for?" Thinking he was the gardener, she said, "Sir, if you have carried him away, tell me where you have put him, and I will get him." Jesus said to her, "Mary."

John 20:15,16 (NIV)

Mary was crying. It had been three days since her world had been turned upside down by the death of her beloved Jesus. Now the disappearance of his body from the borrowed tomb had reopened the fountains of her grief. Down her cheeks streamed hot tears. So heavy was her grief that, at first, she didn't even recognize the risen Lord as he stood behind her that glorious Easter day.

Notice what Jesus didn't say to Mary. He didn't tell her, "Stop crying." Instead, he asked, "Why are you crying?" Her reason seemed real; her loss immense; her tears justified. But then through the fog of her grief and the mist of her tears, she heard him speak again. "Mary," the risen Savior said to her. Only one word. But, oh, how he said it! The love with which he spoke her name brought an end to her tears and gave hope for the future.

Of course we cry when we lose a loved one. Whether it finally comes after a long siege or suddenly strikes out of the blue, a loved one's death stops us in our tracks. How can we go on without that spouse or child or parent at our side? How can we even think of picking up the pieces when life has been so severely shattered? What else can we do but cry? And those tears are important. They are the means God designed for us to release the inner pain and relieve the inner hurt. Sooner or later the tears need to come. And the sooner the better for us.

Mary's tears flowed for three days until she heard her Savior's voice and saw his loving face. For us, the time span may vary. But the antidote is always the same. When the risen Savior's voice breaks through the fog of our grief, the bitterness will drain from our tears. Only then will we be able to view our loved one's loss as victory.

So let the tears come. But don't let them block out the risen Savior's voice as he asks with loving concern, "Why are you crying?" and comforts us with the assurance, "Your loved one lives, with me, in heaven."

Prayer

Lord, you know how hollow I feel and how deeply I'm hurting. My loved one is gone. What am I going to do? How can I go on? Please, Lord, through your promises, show me your loving face and speak to me with your caring voice. Send your Spirit to take the bitterness out of my tears with your promise that those who die with faith in you have eternal life. Amen.

2

Jesus Knows

"Now is your time of grief, but I will see you again and you will rejoice, and no one will take away your joy."

John 16:22 (NIV)

She was too numb to do anything other than go through the motions. Sudden death had ripped her husband from her side. Robbed of the one she loved so dearly, she withdrew inside herself. While making the burial arrangements, visiting with friends at the funeral home, and sitting through the church service, she had maintained her composure fairly well. Later that evening she broke down. "What's wrong with me?" she sobbed in the stillness of her empty home. "Why am I falling apart?"

Nothing was wrong. The grief process is very normal. It's not a sign of weakness or a lack of faith. Rather, grief is the price tag on love. The more we love, the higher the cost. How can we pretend that nothing is wrong? How can we just keep rolling along in life when we've lost loved ones? Regardless of whom we've lost or how they were taken, grief will come. There is no healing without it. Just as the rainbow comes only after the shower has fallen, so healing comes only after grief's pain.

Nor can anyone tell me how to grieve. It's a process that, like our fingerprints, is unique to each one of us. How long my tears will flow, in what way the grief will show, how fast the healing will come—the answers to those questions will vary for each one of us. The old cliché spoken by friends, "I know what you're going through," just doesn't cut it when they are talking about my grief.

But Jesus does know. He showed that as he talked with his disciples the night before his death. Shocked by his announcement that he would die, then numbed beyond belief by his Good Friday cross, they could only huddle behind locked doors, each one of them lost in his grief. And Jesus understood. "Now is your time of grief," he had told them. But he also promised that he would see them again and that their joy would be far greater than their present grief. On Easter Sunday the joy of seeing their risen Savior lifted their grief and lit up their lives.

Jesus knows! He understands how I feel. How hollow I am inside just thinking of life without my loved one. How insecure about going on alone. And he has words for me— promises that will slowly and surely lift grief's fog. Just as he walked through the valley of the shadow of death with my loved one, so he will walk with me. Just as he ushered my loved one into heaven's perfect joy, so he will bring joy back to me. When he walks with me, I will still grieve. But only for a time—and never alone!

Prayer

Jesus, I just don't understand. Why do I feel so numb? Why do I cry so much? In the midst of my grief, let me see your loving face. Tell me again and again, through your Word, that you are with me and that all will be well. Turn my sorrow into joy by reminding me of the eternal life that my loved one now enjoys. Then help me anticipate sharing that joy myself. Amen.

3

IT STILL HURTS

"Even to your old age and gray hairs I am he, I am he who will sustain you. I have made you and I will carry you; I will sustain you and I will rescue you."

Isaiah 46:4 (NIV)

I had prayed for her to go. It's no fun watching your 98-year-old mother fade away, her body worn out and her mind so weary. No fun seeing her limbs so thin and her spirits so tired. During the 40-mile drive home from the hospital, I prayed silently that the Lord would take her home.

So why did I cry when the call came later that night? Wasn't that what I had asked for? Yes, but I couldn't escape my feeling of loss. That was my dear mother, who had carried me under her heart and had given me life at the risk of her own. My dear mother, who had nursed my tiny body at her breast and nourished my young soul on her knees. My dear mother, who was the first to teach me about life—and even more important, about eternal life. My dear mother, whom I sometimes forgot in my eagerness to go about my own life, and to whose house I didn't return often enough.

She was gone. And I was crying. In fact, the tears are still near when, in my mind, I see her face and think of what she meant to me. Regardless of how long we've had loved ones in our lives, losing them still hurts. Regardless of how hard we might have prayed that the Lord take them home, the tears still come when it happens.

Know what I'm talking about, you who have lost loved ones? The tears may come at different times and the loss show in different ways, but you know how it still hurts. Better yet, along with me, you know where to find your comfort—in the God whom Isaiah quoted in our verse. What better comfort can we have than to see the almighty arms of our gracious God cradling our loved ones? Those arms which carried my mother throughout her 98 years were strong when she was weak. They were forgiving when she sinned. They were wrapped around her when she breathed her last. The nail wounds in Jesus' hands guaranteed her safe passage from this vale of tears to her eternal home with him.

It still hurts and always will. But what if we didn't have the comforting assurance of those eternal arms? How much worse our hurt would be.

Prayer

Lord, you know how I hurt because of my loved one's death—and how my pain lingers. I praise you for the blessings you gave my loved one on earth and those you now give in heaven. Help me look back and appreciate the blessings you gave me through that special person. And help me look ahead and anticipate the blessings you will give us both at your side. Dry my tears with your ever-present love. In your name I ask these things. Amen.

4

THE BEST IS YET TO COME

Sarah lived to be a hundred and twenty-seven years old. She died . . . and Abraham went to mourn for Sarah and to weep over her. Then Abraham rose from beside his dead wife and spoke to the Hittites. He said, "I am an alien and a stranger among you. Sell me some property for a burial site here so I can bury my dead."

Genesis 23:1-4 (NIV)

Abraham was crying. Never before and never again does Scripture record an instance when the "father of the faithful" cried. Kneeling beside the form of his beloved wife, Sarah, he was face-to-face with life's greatest sorrow. What a flood of memories must have washed over him! Memories of their common faith, their hopes, their fears, and their joys. What a host of questions must have rushed into his mind. What was he going to do without that trusty partner, that faithful companion at his side? And every memory, every question, must have brought a fresh round of tears.

Can there be anything more painful than the death of a spouse? Gone, never to return, is the one who not only stood at my side but was truly part of me. My arms reach for my lover but come up empty. My heart longs for my confidante but finds no familiar, sympathetic ear. My life needs to go on, but how can I—so all alone? Everywhere I turn, I see her. Every decision I make, I need her. Every day

I live, I miss her. Emotions and memories are not some lifeless objects that can be shoved into a box and stored out of sight. They stay with us all through life.

So I mourn along with Abraham.

My tears don't betray a lack of faith. Rather they are a visible display of my love. Nor is my grief, regardless of how long it runs its course, a sign of my failure to trust God's promises. Instead, it is the process required to mourn my loss, even as I appreciate my loved one's gain.

Death does bring gain for our loved ones. "I am an alien and a stranger among you," Abraham told the Hittites from whom he bought the burial plot for his wife. The father of the faithful knew that he was an outsider—not just among the Hittites, but anywhere on this earth. Heaven was his real home. This side of heaven, he could only be an alien. But now his wife, Sarah, was home. Her soul was enjoying heaven's full citizenship, while her body rested in Canaan's grave.

We cry because of our deep loss. We cry because of our memories. We cry because of the prospect of lonely days ahead. But we do not cry for our loved ones. Those at home in heaven know no tears, only fullness of joy. They suffer no loneliness with the loving Savior always at their side. With this blessed assurance, God comforts us, even as we wait for the best that is yet to come.

Prayer

Lord, I know you understand my tears. You shed them too at the grave of loved ones like Lazarus. Lord, show me the answer for my tears. Comfort me by reminding me of all the blessings I shared with my spouse on earth and by raising my blurry eyes to heaven, where the best is yet to come. Amen.

5

IN SAFE HANDS

My times are in your hands.

Psalm 31:15 (NIV)

We just don't understand, Lord. You know how much we wanted our child. We had a name picked, a room painted, a future all planned for our baby. We could hardly wait till we could cradle it in our arms, cuddle it with our love, care for it with all we had. We were so looking forward to bringing our baby to Baptism, raising it in your name, readying it to share heaven with you and with us.

And now our baby is gone. Taken from us before it could see the light of day. "Miscarriage," the doctor labeled it. If it had happened at birth, "stillborn" would have been his word for it. But those words don't answer our questions or lessen our grief. Why, Lord? We just have to ask. Why, when there are so many unwanted children in the world, did you take the one we wanted so much? Why, when there are so many parents who shirk their responsibilities, did you deny us the privilege we so desired? Why, when so many little ones are raised as heathens, did you take from us the child we were so eager to raise as your very own?

The doctor tried to calm us with statistics about how common miscarriages are. But this was our baby. Relatives tried to console us by saying, "You can always have another one." But we wanted this child. Friends tried to comfort us. "Perhaps there was something wrong with the baby," they would offer. But that didn't help. All we know is that our baby is gone.

Lord, we can't understand. Try as we might, this side of heaven, we'll never be able to search your wisdom completely or to see all your ways clearly. So, please, help us see your loving hands, as King David confessed in the words of his psalm. Help us trust that as your nail-pierced hands once prepared eternal life, they now always protect earthly life. Your loving hands hold the length and breadth of every life—King David's, our own, and our child's. They both create and take back earthly life without always telling us why, except to point to your love.

Let your love—both for our little one and for us—sustain us in these difficult times, till in heaven it answers our question, "Why?"

Prayer

Lord, we know that little ones belong to you and that you love them. Help us to trust that love as we mourn the loss of our baby. Comfort us with the knowledge that you not only hold our lives in your hands but that you also know what's best for your children. Bring healing to our wounded hearts, and raise our eyes to heaven, where one day you will answer our questions in full. Amen.

6

WHY THE CHILDREN?

Now if we are children, then we are heirs—heirs of God and co-heirs with Christ, if indeed we share in his sufferings in order that we may also share in his glory.

Romans 8:17 (NIV)

Do we ever get used to death? We learn to accept it. It's one of those unchangeable facts of life. "The old must die and the young may," we repeat. The first part, about the old dying, we agree with. But not the second. When the young die, it hurts. They're supposed to run and jump and have fun. They're supposed to grow up and be the future after we're gone. Not suffocate in their cribs and be Sudden Infant Death Syndrome statistics. Not get sick, have cancer, and fade away. Not get hurt in accidents, lie in a coma, and finally expire. They're too precious for that.

Our child is a person to whom we gave life. And we would be willing to give our own lives to save our child from death. Our child comes from us, carries our blood, is considered our replacement. To have a child wrenched from us so soon seems all wrong. It's like starting a sentence but not completing it, taking a photo but not developing it, lighting a candle but not letting it burn. "Lord, why our child?" we ask as we feel so helpless, so numb, even so angry. What's the logic in such a death? Where's some meaning that makes some sense?

The Lord has answers for us. Eventually his Spirit causes those answers to take hold of our grieving hearts. "That was really my child," he tells us, "a future heir of my heaven. I only loaned the child to you, to care for in my place. And when I considered your job done, I took my child back. Just as I sent that child from heaven, so I took it back to heaven—but only after using you to prepare the child through the miracle of my love in Baptism and the Word."

"Consider also," he reminds us, "the glory that your child enjoys in heaven. Glory that you still have to wait for. Glory that human words can't really describe. Glory that comes because of Jesus." To see the Savior face-to-face, to stand in the sunshine of his love, to sing his praises—heaven offers all that and more. Compared to heaven's splendor, don't earth's pains and problems seem so trivial? Compared to heaven's glory, doesn't even the loss of a dear child become bearable?

Why the children? Only God can handle that anguished question. May he help us accept what he has already told us in his Word, until that day when he answers all our questions in heaven.

Prayer

Lord, we just don't understand. How could you take our child away from us? Lord, you know that we need to hear again and again that this child was really your child. That you had a glorious place prepared for your child through Jesus' wondrous work of salvation. Keep speaking those truths to our aching hearts. In Jesus' name, to whom all children are precious, we ask it. Amen.

7

TELL ME AGAIN

"Be still and know that I am God."

Psalm 46:10 (NIV)

I still can't believe it. As he hurried out the door on his way to work, he promised to bring the dry cleaning home. Now he's gone. The police came first and then the pastor. "Horrible accident," they said. But their words barely sunk in. "Death was quick," they comforted. But that didn't mean much. "Let us know if you need anything," they offered. But I didn't even know what I needed.

"It can't be. They must be wrong," I reacted first, doubting the truth. "It shouldn't be," came next, as I got upset over what seemed so unfair. "Why'd you let it be?" I even said, looking up in anger at God. Time has passed. Yet so many of those same feelings resurface when I walk into my husband's workshop, wrestle alone with raising the kids, and weep in our bedroom at night.

Tell me again what God says. No, he doesn't promise me all sunshine and no storm. He doesn't say that he'll unroll all the answers and unravel all the questions. But he does encourage me, "Be still." He does remind me, "Know that I am God." When the wrecking ball of trouble shatters our lives, it's not because God has sent it to the wrong places. When the volcanoes of disaster engulf our homes, it's not because he has forgotten our house numbers. God is there, even when we think he isn't. God knows what he's doing, even when we don't. He says, "Be still and know that I am God."

Someday, when eternity enfolds me, all the mysteries in my life, including this one, will become clear. But I'm still living on this side of heaven. So I need to hear again and again what my gracious God has said. Tell me he knows why I feel so angry and resentful, even though I should know better. How can I find peace unless he forgives me? Tell me he knows how deep my sorrow is, how it threatens to drown me every day. How can I learn to smile again, unless he comforts me? Tell me he knows that my many practical questions about the days ahead seem to have no answers. How can I keep putting one foot ahead of the other unless he takes my hand and leads me? Remind me of his promise that I will see my loved one in heaven along with all other believers in Christ. How can I be assured of this unless he builds my faith in his Son, whom he sent to remove my sins and to ready me for heaven?

Please, Lord, eternal helper of the helpless, keep telling me, "Be still and know that I am God."

Prayer

Lord, I need your presence every passing hour, especially in the time of sudden loss and grief. To whom can I turn, but you? Where can I find relief, but in your arms? Bring me comfort through your promise that you are always here with your power. Help me to trust what I can't yet understand, that your love always makes everything turn out good for your children. Amen.

8

HOW WEAK WE ARE!

As a father has compassion on his children, so the LORD
has compassion on those who fear him; for he knows
how we are formed, he remembers that we are dust.

Psalm 103:13,14 (NIV)

The call came shortly after midnight, from the university
miles away. A 20-year-old son had taken his own life. What
a shock! Ordinary death brings enough agony in its wake.
How much more so when it is suicide. By a single act, suicide casts a lingering pall over the whole family.

No, that young man's death was not God's will. Life is
the time a gracious God gives every human being to prepare for heaven. And no one but the giver of life has the
right to end that time of grace, either for oneself or for others. Those who ignore God's gracious will should be ready
for the just consequences.

Serious concerns about the young man's eternal future
lingered on. As did the feelings of hurt, guilt, even anger.
Why didn't our son love us enough to talk about his problems? How are we going to tell the rest of the family and
our friends? What will they think about our son and us
when they hear the word *suicide?* Why didn't we see this
coming? Why didn't we read more into the long intervals
between his calls home—and his silence when he did come

home? Why did he do this to us? How could he hurt us so much? And how could God allow this hurt to happen?

The Lord knows how weak we are, how much like the dust that swirls aimlessly around. He also knew our son. God knew everything that was going on in his mind. He knows that, like an arm twisted in the wrong direction, a mind can snap. To God's judgment we commit our son. He, the compassionate Father, knows all the circumstances. And he will judge accordingly.

To that compassionate Father, we also need to commit ourselves. Family and friends can close ranks around us. They can offer us a measure of support and strength. But nothing like what the heavenly Father can offer,. In the atoning blood of his Son, he helps us find the pardon we need for any neglect toward our son or any anger now toward him or toward God. In the strength of God's love we find the power we need, in the midst of our grief, to go forward into the future.

Frail children of dust we are, very much so. But God is still the compassionate Father of his children. Our Father too!

Prayer

Loving Father, we have so many questions and so few answers. Help us leave our loved one's eternal future in your just hands. Help us lay our hurting hearts in your lap, knowing that you, our compassionate Father, care for us. Grant us the pardon, peace, and power we need to go forward, even in the midst of our grief. In Jesus' name we come to you. Amen.

9

A Very Special Friend

When the Lord saw her, his heart went out to her
and he said, "Don't cry." Then he went up and
touched the coffin, and those carrying it stood still.
He said, "Young man, I say to you, get up!" The dead
man sat up and began to talk, and Jesus gave him
back to his mother.

Luke 7:13-15 (NIV)

Friends and relatives trudged with her that day to the
cemetery. But what could they really do to dilute her tears
and lift her fears? Robbed, first of her husband and now her
son, that widow was really all alone. Sympathetic words
could take the edge off but not eliminate her grief. Kind
gestures showed they cared. But she still had to carry the
burden of a lonely future.

I think I know how she must have felt. I can't really
remember who all was there or what they all said. But I was
glad they were there. Their presence at my side helped to
ease my pain and keep me going in those dark hours. The
death of a loved one is truly a time when we need friends
and relatives.

Death is certainly a time when I need my very special
friend, the one the widow met that day, the one I have
known for some time. What a friend Jesus is in death's dark

hour. This special friend truly feels my pain. He cries when he sees my tears. He understands when I sob in fear. He's been through it all himself—the agony of his cross, the reality of his tomb. But with his death and resurrection, he cut death down to size. With his full payment for sin, he shattered death's chains, sealed hell's doors, and swung the gates of heaven wide open. As I walk through death's valley, the shadows may still be dark, but I no longer dread them—because of my special friend.

Into Jesus' caring hands, I can commit my spouse, my child, or my parent when the time comes that they must leave. For a loved one who dies with faith in him, Jesus does even greater things than he did for the widow's son. He ushers the believer's soul, not back to some home on earth, but to the Father's house above. On the Last Day when he again says, "Get up," my loved one's body will rise just as surely as the young man's at Nain did.

Jesus is my very special friend. His strong arms wrap me close when sobs convulse my body. His gentle hands dry my tears. His life-giving Word works the peace my anxious heart needs.

Come, divine friend, Stay with me and never leave.

Prayer

What a friend I have in Jesus! Be with me, precious Savior, and comfort my aching heart. Without your words of forgiveness and life, I would have no peace. With them, I can face my loss, knowing my loved one has gained. With them, I can also face the future, unknown as it may seem. Be with me today and always. Amen.

10

WHERE DID GRANDPA GO?

We . . . would prefer to be away from the body and at home with the Lord.

2 Corinthians 5:8 (NIV)

How do I tell my children about their grandfather's death? Death is one of the most difficult topics to explain to children. What should I say when they come down to breakfast? They'll ask about Grandpa, and I'll have to tell them.

They do know something about death. When we had our dog put down, they learned about loss and absence. When their pet rabbit died, they saw how stiff it was as they helped bury it in the garden.

But Grandpa's different. We don't just put him in the ground. He went to sleep, but unlike my children's pets, he's going to wake up again. Because he is God's child, he's already in a special place, at home with the Lord in heaven. How do I explain, though—that's the question. If I say "We lost Grandpa today," the kids will ask, "Where can we find him?" If I take them to the funeral, they'll question, "What's Grandpa doing in that shiny box?" If they touch his cheek, they'll wonder, "Why is he so cold?" Please, Lord, help me explain.

Didn't Paul give us a hint when he wrote about being away from the body and at home with the Lord? Aren't our bodies something like houses in which our souls live?

"What's a soul?" my children ask. Well, it's a part of us we can't see. Part of us that also laughs and cries, that loves God and wants to be like him. The part of us that goes to heaven when we die. Last night God called Grandpa's soul home to heaven. So he went. But he left his body behind, like a house in which he had been staying. Grandpa doesn't need his body anymore. So we'll place it in the ground, believing that God will put it back together one day so that Grandpa can use it again in heaven.

"Heaven? What's heaven like?" If I say a place of rest, that won't mean much to the children. If I answer, perfect joy, that's way too abstract for little minds. Perhaps I can use pictures to describe Grandpa's joy in heaven. How it's like if he could fish all the time. They'll remember how he loved to fish. How it's like if his favorite team would win all the time. They will understand that. How it's like if he never had to go to the hospital bed again. They would agree. They need to hear about heaven's joy and rest in terms they can feel and grasp.

And don't let me forget to tell them who took Grandpa to heaven. Every night they pray, "If I should die before I wake, I pray the Lord my soul to take. And this I ask for Jesus' sake." So did their grandpa. They know what Jesus meant to him. They know what Jesus did for him. They'll believe that because of Jesus, they'll see Grandpa again in heaven.

Prayer

Lord, give me the words to use with my children so that they can understand heaven's joy and rest. Give me the faith of a little child so that I can rejoice with them over my loved one's gain. So that I can look forward to the blessed reunion in heaven. Amen.

11

ANSWER FOR ANGER

My soul is in anguish. How long, O LORD, how long?
Turn, O LORD, and deliver me; save me because of
your unfailing love.

Psalm 6:3,4 (NIV)

Is it wrong for me to be angry? I know, Lord, that
Christians should believe that in all things you work for our
good. I know that Christians should trust you to lead cor-
rectly. We should leave the future in your hands. I know
what I should be and do, but I can't. Inside me bitterness
smolders like a volcano and erupts into anger before I can
stop it.

Sometimes I even get angry at you, Lord. How could you
have done this to me? Didn't you know our plans—the
future we had laid out so carefully together? You suppos-
edly control all things, but you didn't seem to care enough
about our plans. Can you understand, Lord, how I feel—
how cheated and disappointed?

I also get angry with those around me. When will my
relatives stop asking how I feel? When will my friends stop
pressing me to get on with my life, as if my loss were just
a momentary distraction? When will it be easier for me to
look at those people who hurt my loved one in the past and
now act as if nothing ever happened? Can you understand,

Lord, how I have to bite my tongue at times? And, at other times, why I just have to snap back at them?

And I get angry with myself. When I recall the moments I wasted, the things I said or didn't say, the love I didn't show, I just have to cry. How could I have been so selfish and unconcerned? Can you understand, Lord, why some memories hurt and why I get down on myself?

Tell me that you understand. Remind me that you are my Creator, who has endowed me with feelings. Assure me that when death snatches a loved one away, the emotion we call anger is natural. Help me understand anger's role in venting my grief and heading me toward healing. But, above all, forgive me when my anger becomes sin. When it is laced with bitter resentment against your will and selfish pity for myself or when it is my sinful reaction toward my neighbor, hold your unfailing love before my eyes. Point me again to your Son's cross and his precious blood, with which your love canceled the guilt of all my sins. Let your unfailing love be the answer for my anger and my grief.

Prayer

Lord, sometimes I can't hold my anger in. I wonder about your ways, worry about my future, and weary under my prolonged grief. Help me sort through my feelings and understand anger's role. Turn me to your Son's cross and the healing it offers when I sin in my anger. Help me trust your unfailing love in the days ahead as I continue to heal. Amen.

12

FEELING GUILTY?

I trust in your unfailing love; my heart rejoices in your salvation.

Psalm 13:5 (NIV)

"If only I had called 9-1-1 sooner," June lamented to her pastor. She had wanted to call as soon as her husband woke her. But that was 2:00 A.M., and the pains weren't steady, so they delayed. Too late she had reached for the phone—her husband never made it to the hospital.

"If only!" What spirit-crushing words those are. If only I had called sooner. If only I had been at the hospital when mother died. If only I could go back and recall those sharp words, rescind those angry outbursts, and undo those hurt-ful actions. Those two words, if only, hang around our necks like a ton of guilt. If not dealt with, they can even choke us.

Feelings of guilt over the loss of a loved one aren't unusual. How can two sinful human beings live side by side without hurting each other? How can I live day by day with my spouse and never have anything go wrong? In fact, part of the richness in marriage comes from forgiving each other and reconciling after the hurt. But feelings of guilt are normal. They come because we are sinners.

Then there's the guilt that we load upon ourselves. Of course we want to take good care of our loved ones.

Of course we want to be with them when they breathe their last. But who do we think we are? Have we forgotten that God, not we, is in control of life? Our presence at the bedside might have provided some comfort, but could it postpone that last breath? Sin is not always behind such assumed guilt, but it weighs heavily all the same.

Wisely the pastor let June express her guilt. Then, as her tears subsided and her words slowed, he pointed her to Jesus. "Your Savior knows," he said. "He knows how guilty you feel, and he forgives you. On the cross he paid for all your sins, including those you feel so guilty about right now. We can't go back and undo what we have done in life, nor do we have to. We have trouble forgetting, but God doesn't remember. He has plunged our sins into the depths of the sea. And now they're gone as if they never happened." Then he concluded, "Once we know the joy of his forgiveness, we can forgive ourselves and deal with our other feelings too."

Feeling guilty? Is there any better answer than the prayer, "Lord, help me trust in your unfailing love and rejoice in your salvation"?

Prayer

Thank you, Lord, for listening to me. Help me listen to your promises so that I trust your love and rejoice in your salvation. Amen.

13

RUNNING ON EMPTY

When my spirit grows faint within me, it is you who know my way.

Psalm 142:3 (NIV)

"Why am I so tired all the time?" she worried. "Why don't I feel like doing anything?" Her husband's illness had been a long siege. From diagnosis, to surgery, to the treatments, and then through weeks of wasting away, more than nine long months had crept by. Every day she had been at her husband's side. Every night, when he was still home, she would wake up, straining to hear if he was still breathing. Strength was her middle name, at least out in public. Although she didn't know it, her energy tank had been emptied, and she was running on the fumes.

Now all she had left of her loved one was that bare spot out at the cemetery. He was gone and so was her reason to keep going. And she collapsed. It was as if she had run full speed into a brick wall and was lying there semiconscious. Some nights she couldn't get to sleep. Some days she couldn't seem to wake up. Halfheartedly she poked around at what needed to be done; lackadaisically she picked at her food. "What's wrong with me?" she wondered. "Why can't I get my life going again?"

Those who lose loved ones often experience physical distress. The more prolonged the ordeal and the deeper the loss, the greater such physical distress can be. Our physical side is so intertwined with the emotional that what happens to the one affects the other. When the spirit within grows faint, the body without feels it too. If our physical problems are real, they loom larger. If they are imagined, they still seem real. A trip to the doctor and an appropriate prescription may be necessary. So is time: time for our spirits to recharge and our bodies to recoup. No one can set a timetable for such recharging. We all grieve according to our own personal clocks.

But each of us can look to the Lord. "You know my way," the psalmist said, looking up at his gracious God. The Lord's sympathetic ear is always ready to listen when my grieving heart overflows. His loving heart always understands when my spirit cries out in anguish. His almighty arm is always ready to cradle me when my tank has run empty.

Sharing my concerns with friends can release a fraction of grief's pressure. Carrying them to the Lord brings what I need for soul and body. From him comes the hope I need for the loved one I've lost. From him comes also the help I need to get my life back on track. Lord, help me let go of the feeling that I must stand alone. Help me lean on you.

Prayer

Lord, I don't know if I can go on. Where can I turn? What can I do? Help me realize that my body feels my loss too. Above all, anchor my spirit in your strength. Hold me up with your promises of eternal life and your promises to help with earthly life. Remind me that these promises were there for my loved one, as they are now here for me. Amen.

14

THEY JUST DON'T KNOW

He who did not spare his own Son, but gave him up for us all—how will he not also, along with him, graciously give us all things?

Romans 8:32 (NIV)

"They just don't know!" he suddenly exclaimed. "How can they know what we're feeling? How can they know how much it hurts?" It was two weeks after the funeral of his teenage son. The father was sitting in the pastor's study, discussing how they would use the many memorial gifts they had received. All at once he stopped, his eyes shining with hot tears, his heart spilling out his heavy grief.

His son had died in a tragic car accident. Well-intentioned people offered comfort. The line at the funeral home was long, the concern genuine, the sympathy heartfelt. Many didn't know what to say. Some tried to console him, "We know what you must be feeling." But how could they? No matter whom others have lost or under what circumstances, they can't really understand. Even if they've lost a 17-year-old son, a spouse, or a parent, this is still his loved one, not theirs. And it's his pain!

The pastor quickly came around from behind his desk and put his arm on that grieving father's shoulder. "You're right," he said softly. "Nobody can really know your pain.

Nobody," he continued, "except the Lord. He too had a Son, one whom he dearly loved. And he lost that Son. Or we should say, he gave up that Son. He sent him down to this earth, put our human skin around him, put our many sins upon him, put him on a cross—into hell's depths—and even into a grave to pay for those sins. God loved his only begotten Son dearly, but he also loved us. And in that awesome love, he gave his Son into death for us."

Friends and relatives can only guess at my pain. God knows. His divine love always knows. It knew what was good for my loved one. It knows what is good for me. It cries and rejoices with me when I lose a loved one and that loved one gains heaven. When God puts his hand on my shoulder and says, "I know how you feel," I know he really does. When he says, "Let me help you," I know he can. When he says, "Let me lead you," I know he will—over life's bumps and bruises, to the heaven he has prepared by giving up his own Son.

Paul said it so well. May God help me believe that the love which caused him to give me his own Son will also give me what I need, even at a painful time like this.

Prayer

Thank you, Lord, for your heart of love and the Son it gave for me. Comfort me in my loss with your love. Dry my tears, lift my spirits, and warm my heart with the sure touch of your loving hand as it reaches out to me through your Word. Amen.

15

NEVER ALONE

"Surely I am with you always, to the very end of the age."

Matthew 28:20 (NIV)

"I know," said the widow. "I'm never alone. But it's so hard without him." They had been married for 51 years. Together they had walked life's path. From newlyweds just starting out to great-grandparents, they had faced the ups and downs of life together. "Oh, yes," she reminisced, "we had our arguments and troubles, but it was always so much fun making up. How I wish I could see him and talk to him," she would lament wistfully. "I'm so lonely without him."

In her heart, the grieving widow knew the correct answer for her loneliness. In the funeral sermon, she had heard her pastor state: "You will feel so alone in the days and weeks ahead. But remember you're never alone. At your side will be Jesus—minute after minute, day after day, week after week. He promised to be with you always. And he is— even though at times it's hard to see him because grief's loss and sorrow's tears blur your sight."

How lonely the loss of a loved one makes me feel. Never again to be able to hug or kiss him. Never again to hear his voice. Never again to laugh and cry with him. Instead, his place is empty at the table, in the car, and in my life. His clothes still hang in our bedroom closet. Our anniversary picture still stands on the dresser. Traces of him are still present everywhere. But he's not here. All I have left is my aching sense of loss and my heartbreaking loneliness.

Just think what life would be like without Jesus' presence. If, in the midst of aching loss, I couldn't say, "But I know I'm never alone." If Jesus had never spoken his promise, how endless my tears would be, how complete my loneliness. But my Jesus has promised to be with me always. When, like Peter, I'm threatened by the waves of life, Jesus will pull me into the boat with him. When, like Mary and Martha, I'm swamped by the losses of life, Jesus will speak words of eternal life to me. When, like the disciples in the wilderness, my five barley loaves and two small fish seem insufficient for the future, Jesus will bless them and make them stretch.

You promised, Lord Jesus. Now help me believe that I am never alone.

Prayer

Lord Jesus, please brush aside my tears so that I can clearly see that you are at my side. Bring me back again and again to your beautiful promise, "Surely I am with you always." Let your abiding presence be my strength and comfort in these difficult days. Amen.

16

THE RAINBOW OF GOD'S LOVE

Hope does not disappoint us, because God has poured out his love into our hearts by the Holy Spirit, whom he has given us.

Romans 5:5 (NIV)

What a beautiful rainbow! Driving across Montana's big sky country, we had run into a rainstorm. When I could finally turn off the windshield wipers, a rainbow arched across the sky ahead of us, with all its brilliant colors. How much like the journey of life. A storm can come so suddenly and stay so long. We drive, sometimes it seems for miles, under a dark sky and through a dense downpour. But then the storm lifts, the sun shines, and a rainbow appears ahead.

The rainbow of God's love we might call it. It comes at the end of the storm, and it reflects from my tears. Right now I may see only the storm. I may flinch as the lightning bolts of sorrow pierce my heart, as the grief thunders through my soul. Perhaps I've already been traveling for miles in the storm, and I don't seem to be driving out of it. But I know that the rainbow of God's love shines up ahead. Sooner or later I'll see the brilliant colors of his love arching over my loss.

Do I miss my loved one? Of course I do—and always will. But rainbow time is coming, and God's love shines on my tears with his promise, "I am the resurrection and the life. He who believes in me will live, even though he dies" (John 11:25).

Am I afraid as I look ahead? Of course I am. But God never asks his children to walk where he doesn't lead. Rainbow time lies ahead, and God's love eases my fears with his promise, "Never will I leave you; never will I forsake you" (Hebrews 13:5).

Will I get over my loss? No, but I'll learn to live with it. Rainbow time awaits, and God's love promises that I will be reunited with fellow believers at his side in heaven. His love will bind up my troubled heart every time some memory or anniversary rips loose the scab that passing time has patched over my hurt.

Slowly, yet surely, the storm will pass and the rainbow of God's love will appear in life's sky. The Holy Spirit, whom God sends to work faith in my fainting heart, will keep this hope alive even in my loss. He uses my tears to reflect the rainbow of God's love even more brilliantly.

Prayer

Lord, I can't see very far right now. My tears are heavy, and my loss is great. Send your Spirit to assure me that at the end of the storm stands the rainbow of your love. Fill me with the sure hope that your love governs all things for my good so that I might have the courage to continue walking through this storm. Amen.

17

ONE DAY AT A TIME

The LORD watches over you.

Psalm 121:5 (NIV)

"I just can't go on like this," the husband spoke from his chair in the pastor's study. Ever since he and his wife had lost their little boy, home life had been bleak. While their six-year-old had been fighting for his life in Children's Hospital, they had pulled together. Now, with their son gone, they seemed to be pulling apart. Both mourned his death deeply, each in his or her own way. Both felt guilty, as if God should have taken the parent in place of the child. Both harbored resentment, as if cheated out of the future. The father plunged into his work as an outlet for his grief. The mother bottled up her grief, drifting around the house as if in a trance, weeping frequently, neglecting the rest of the family.

Death brings stress and exerts a lot of pressure on those who mourn. Sometimes cracks appear in the family structure. Particularly with the death of a child. Such a loss tests a marriage as little else can.

After listening to the husband, the pastor offered some valuable advice. First he scheduled the man and his wife for counseling. Then he wrote five words on a slip of paper and encouraged the couple to read them together each day.

Only five simple words, but packed with meaning: "The LORD watches over you." The pastor even suggested changing one word. "When you read the verse," he said, "read 'The LORD watches over us.'"

Like that grieving couple, I need to know that the Lord hasn't forgotten me but that he is right here. And that he has whatever I need. He was with Jairus when his daughter slept in death. With the widow of Nain when her son's body was carried out of the village. With Mary and Martha as they mourned for their brother. But I need him for my loss. I need to know he's watching over *me* in my time of grief. How can I take even one step on the road to healing unless he's at my side? How can I face tomorrow unless he helps me?

Without my gracious Lord I can't face today, much less tomorrow. With him watching over me, I can move forward one day at a time.

Prayer

Be near me, Lord Jesus. I ask you to stay close by me forever and love me, I pray. Hear my prayer, dear Jesus, and keep me in my hour of grief. With your loving promises, strengthen me so that I can put one foot ahead of the other as I journey into tomorrow. Amen.

18

CHANGING CHAPTERS IN LIFE

Because of the LORD's great love we are not consumed, for his compassions never fail. They are new every morning; great is your faithfulness.

Lamentations 3:22,23 (NIV)

Two chapters cover our lives—before and after. One we can change; the other we need to accept. The distinction between these two chapters is particularly visible when a loved one dies.

When a loved one dies, the "before" chapter holds the memories of the good times we had together. Recalling the past, looking at the photos, and laughing at the pranks, I appreciate the blessing God gave me through my loved one. But I can't recreate those scenes, much as I would want to.

In the before chapter, I also revisit the hurts of the past. The quarrels I never resolved, my stubborn, selfish actions, the opportunities to love I let pass by—they all keep scrolling up on my memory's screen, and I can't seem to delete them. But I can't go back and redo them either, no matter how much I want to.

As I reread the before chapter, I can react to my past life. We had each other, though we didn't always appreciate what we had. We did things together, though we didn't always realize how much sharing joy and sorrow meant.

Some days were better than others, but even the worst was far better than what I have now. But I can't extend the past, no matter how much I want to.

As I grieve, I can't help turning back to the before chapter of life. But sooner or later I have to turn to the chapter entitled "after." And the sooner the better. Each day in this chapter is a blank page just waiting to be written. Tears may blur my entries, but let the pages show that I'm using my time of grace. Let them show that, though I now read alone, sit alone, and go to Holy Communion alone, I know how God uses his Word and Supper to strengthen my faith and ready me for heaven.

Memories of the past bring back tears. But let my entries in the after chapter show my daily concern for those around me. My family needs my encouragement, neighbors my charity, fellow church members my efforts. Besides, in my family, neighborhood, and world, so many don't have the Savior. They need my efforts, prayers, and offerings.

Moving on to the next chapter in life is not easy. Without the Lord's forgiving love for the past and his compassion for the present, I couldn't do it. With his help I can accept the past and start writing the story of the future

Prayer

Lord, I can't help looking back. When I do, I long for the blessings I once had, and I want to undo the things I did wrong. Please assure me of your forgiving love. Please also cover me with your compassion. Encourage me, enable me, equip me to go forward, with joy over the blessings I still have and with energy for the life you put before me. Amen.

19

WHERE ARE THEY NOW?

"You did not choose me, but I chose you."

John 15:16 (NIV)

They were always there at first. The telephone kept ringing. The cards kept coming. The freezer kept filling up with casseroles. At the funeral home they squeezed my arm and spoke words of sympathy. The week after the funeral, some of them still stopped by and asked what they could do. But now it's quiet. Except for a few close friends and family members, they don't call anymore. I know they have their own lives to live and they expect me to get on with mine. I know they say I'm welcome in their homes, but I don't want to intrude. I know they tell me to call anytime, but I can hear the hesitation when they answer. I can't help wondering where they are now when I still need them.

Thank God for Jesus. What a precious friend he is! His friendship is his gift to me. Just as an abandoned child doesn't choose its adoptive parents, so I didn't pick him. But I wasn't just a sinner, I was his bitter enemy. Yet in love he chose me. If his love hadn't shed his blood on Calvary's cross, I'd still be in my sins—and I'd be an eternity away from his friendship. But my friend didn't ask, "What can I do for you?" He went ahead and did it, paying for my sin and making our eternal friendship possible. That's right, his friendship with me never ends. It has no "shelf life" but lasts into eternity.

My heavenly friend is always there when I need him. Any hour, day or night, I can call on him through my prayers. I don't need a phone number or computer modem, just the confidence that I can approach my Savior boldly with all my needs. Any request, little or large, I can carry to him. I don't have to hesitate or stammer, just remind him of his promise that whatever I asked in his name he will give. Anytime I feel like crying on his shoulder, I can do so. I don't have to fear rebuke or rejection, just believe that he will carry whatever anxiety I cast upon him.

As the weeks pass by, he's still there. When I waver in sin, he wraps his forgiveness around me. When I feel sorry for myself, he shapes me up. When I cry bitter tears, he blots them dry. When I fear the darkness of the future, he floods it with light. And all because of his amazing love.

Friends are important, especially in a time of grief. But none more so than my heavenly friend. Thank you, Jesus, for being my friend.

Prayer

What a friend I have in Jesus! What a privilege to carry everything to him in prayer! Lord, help me appreciate what you have done to enable me to call you friend. Also, help me call on you in my current time of need. For your love's sake, hear and answer me. Amen.

20

FACING THE FIRSTS

"Seek first his kingdom and his righteousness, and all
these things will be given to you as well."

Matthew 6:33 (NIV)

During the four months since his wife's funeral, Pete
hadn't come to the Communion table. Finally he stood
there. When the pastor reached him, Pete's shoulders shook
with silent sobs. After church he explained, "I just couldn't
come. We always went to Communion together. The first
time alone was almost more than I could handle."

After the loss of a loved one, first times alone are difficult. Like the first time back at a favorite restaurant: how
choked up that empty chair can make me feel. Like the first
birthday: there is no need for a cake because no one is there
to blow out the candles. Like the first wedding anniversary:
now the number of years together is frozen by death. Like
the first Christmas: there is no one with whom we can
enjoy God's gift—or share our own. Like the first time
alone on the church bench or at the Communion table:
though faith is an individual matter, it is also shared.

Talk about sudden lumps in the throat and sharp tears
in the eyes! That first year without my loved one can certainly bring them. Each year that follows is better. But that
doesn't ease the pain of that first year.

Jesus speaks of a "first" that helps. Remember to "seek first [my] kingdom," he says. Even in my loss—especially in my loss—I need the forgiveness, the comfort, the peace, the joy Jesus offers me in his kingdom of grace. Your life with your loved one was rich in the treasures of my kingdom, Jesus reminds me. Now don't let tears dim your sight. Don't let loss lead you away. Appreciate what you had together as members of my kingdom. Because of these heavenly treasures, you are able to say a hopeful "See you later" to your loved one, instead of a wrenching "good-bye." Because of the wealth you still have in me, you can face life without your loved one as you look forward to what awaits you also at my eternal side.

Jesus doesn't say it will be easy. But he does make it possible. First his kingdom, he says. Then all these things—including the first year with all its painful firsts.

Prayer

Lord, it's not easy going on alone. So many things remind me of my loved one and rekindle my grief. Help me understand, Lord, that I'm not alone when I feel this pain. Even more, help me raise my eyes in faith to your kingdom. Comfort me with reminders of blessings we enjoyed together as children of your grace, and keep me going with the promise of treasures that await me in heaven. Amen.

21

HOPE FOR GOING ON

No one whose hope is in you [O LORD] will ever be
put to shame.

Psalm 25:3 (NIV)

"I'm beginning to hope again," he told his pastor.
"Yesterday I made it through the grocery store without
fighting tears. Last Sunday I sang all the hymns, even the
one that was her favorite. Maybe now I can have my daughter come over and help me go through my wife's things."

When that widower said *hope*, he picked the right word.
Like an alkaline battery, hope energizes our lives. It turns
the lights on and keeps our daily lives running. When loss
drains hope's battery and sorrow corrodes its contacts, life
slows to a halt. The lights go out in our hearts and our lives.
Each day just seems filled with more of the same darkness.
The future looms like something to be endured, not something that could be enjoyed.

Of course I miss my loved one—and always will. Of
course life is different without her—and always will be. But
I must and I can go on with God as my hope. At first I
thought he had forgotten me or that he was getting even
with me for some sin. I knew better, but that's what grief
can do. It can blot out God's promises and block the sight
of his loving face. But now I'm beginning to appreciate his

goodness, for giving me my loved one all these years. And his grace, for taking her to heaven.

At first I thought I couldn't go on without her. It was as if half of me had been chainsawed away, leaving only bloody wounds. I thought God was playing some sort of trick on me or getting some sadistic kick out of running me through an obstacle course that was too advanced for me. I knew his promises, but grief can make you forget, or even worse, it can cause you to doubt. But now I'm beginning to feel his hand again. It was there all the time, carrying me when I couldn't walk and now encouraging me as I take baby steps forward.

I don't know what tomorrow will bring, maybe two steps forward and one step backward. Most of the time I don't even want to know. But I can be confident of one thing: God will be there to help me. His saving love in Jesus is my sure hope for heaven and my help in life's journey, wherever it leads.

Prayer

Lord, helper of the helpless and hope of the hopeless, take my hand and lead me. Help me walk with increasing confidence in the hope your sure Word offers, for earth and for heaven. Amen.

22

COMPANIONS ALONG THE WAY

The LORD God said, "It is not good for the man to be alone."

Genesis 2:18 (NIV)

The journey over grief's mountain can be a lonely one. From "nobody knows how I feel" to "just leave me alone," I usually walk sorrow's steep path alone. The time comes, though, when I feel again the need for the company of others. That's how God made me, not to exist as isolated as some island, but alongside others, in a marriage, a family, a church, and a community.

"I went back to my card club yesterday," my mother told me over the phone. Six months had to pass before she took that step out of loneliness. All my cajoling along the way did little good. When she had worked partway through my dad's death, she could enjoy her friends again. In fact, she needed their company again to fill her life.

"I've found a nice lady to keep me company," Ed said. He and his wife had been so close. They had built a marriage, a family, and a business together. They had enjoyed each other's company on life's journey. Then cancer had claimed his dear wife. Ed kept going, but the spring was out of his step. He kept doing, but the usual smile was gone. Till that day when he "chanced" into my study with what was really a question. He wasn't just telling me about his lady friend. He was asking if such a relationship were okay. To have someone with whom he could share activities and go places filled his need for companionship with someone of the opposite sex.

"I thought I'd never marry again," recalled Lois. "I remember, Pastor, that when Bill died you said something that made me shake my head no. You said that perhaps God would one day give me a new husband. I thought no one would, or could, ever take Bill's place." Gently the pastor corrected her. "No one will ever take Bill's place," he said. "The memories of your life with him are yours to treasure forever. But those memories should not hold you back from creating new ones. When Bill died, your ability to love did not die with him. The ability to love is God's gift to an individual. And the need to be loved remains with us all our days."

Regardless of how long the journey over grief's mountain takes, Jesus is my closest companion. Without his precious love, I couldn't take one step forward. As I progress on that journey, it's only natural for me to look for other companions too. Through them Jesus also gives me love.

Prayer

Thank you, loving Savior, for keeping me company on sorrow's journey. You've strengthened my feet and brightened my days. Please provide me with the companions I need as I continue the journey. You know what such companions can do for me and how much I need them. Amen.

23

AMAZING GRACE AND ABUNDANT PEACE

Grace and peace be yours in abundance.

1 Peter 1:2 (NIV)

"How did God ever put up with me?" I wonder. All I've done these past months is gripe. Ever since my loved one died, I've been flooding heaven's complaint box. From "How could you do this to me, God?" to "Didn't you know our plans?" I've been grousing about God and to God. How can he love someone like me, someone not only so sinful but also so ungrateful?

The answer, Peter reminds me, is amazing grace. Simply explained, grace is all the undeserved love God lavishes upon me for Jesus' sake. Instead of punishment for my many sins, he gives me pardon. Instead of the hell I have coming, he prepares me for heaven. Instead of well-deserved curses, he showers me with blessings.

Why does he keep doing all this for me? How can he keep blessing me when all I do is fill the air with complaints? How can he keep walking with me when all I do is question his direction? How can he keep nudging me toward heaven when all I do is keep veering toward hell? He must really love me—but I don't know why. The answer has to be grace—his amazing grace.

When I recognize God's grace as I journey along grief's highway, peace finally starts to come. Peace inches into my heart as I look back at the blessings with which God graced life with my loved one. Peace increases as I look forward to the protection with which God will grace my lonely walk into the future. Peace intensifies as I look down at myself and realize that grace has transformed me from hell's fearful citizen to a member of heaven's family circle. My peace grows as I look up at the heaven God's grace has given my loved one and guarantees also for me.

As I trudge through the trials of life, I get to taste God's grace more deeply. As I weep the tears of life, I am drenched with the warm rain of his grace more fully. Those who have made the journey through the valley of loss know that his grace and peace go with them in abundance. Thank God, so do I!

Prayer

Through many dangers, toils, and snares
I have already come;
'Tis grace has brought me safe thus far,
And grace will lead me home.

Lord, let these words be my thanks, my comfort, and my peace. For Jesus' sake. Amen.

24

What's Heaven Like?

"They have washed their robes and made them white in the blood of the Lamb. Therefore, they are before the throne of God. . . . The sun will not beat upon them, nor any scorching heat. For the Lamb at the center of the throne will be their shepherd."

Revelation 7:14-17 (NIV)

"What's heaven like?" children ask and adults wonder. In times of grief, this question rises to the surface. The dying need answers and so do those like me, who mourn the loss of a loved one

What's heaven like? In his grand vision, John gives us some idea. He describes heaven as a place where sin is completely absent. There'll be no more temptation to sin. No more devil or wicked cohorts trying to trick us into sin. No more evil world around us or evil hearts within us, tantalizing us with sin. That's what it means to be dressed in white robes. White symbolizes purity. In heaven we'll be perfectly sinless, like the holy angels.

What's heaven like? No more suffering, John also answers. Here on earth, trouble scorches us relentlessly like the burning desert sun. Affliction sears our souls. But in heaven all suffering and sickness will be gone—all pains and problems, all diseases and defects. Instead, Christ the

Lamb will be there like a shepherd, to lead us into heaven's shade and to refresh our souls.

What's heaven like? Always being with the Lord, John continues in his answer. As we journey through life, we know God is at our side. But we cannot see him with our eyes or touch him with our hands, much as we might long to at times. In heaven we shall. What a day that will be when we see his face, with all its rich love shining forth! What a joy that will be—the fullest joy of heaven—to be face-to-face with our Savior forever!

More important than what heaven is like is the question, Who will be there? Those who "have washed their robes and made them white in the blood of the Lamb," John tells us. Not all people, not even all religious people, will be in heaven. Only those who believe in Jesus Christ as their Savior. Only his holy blood bleaches out sin's tough stain. Only his perfect righteousness dresses us for heaven. Only those who die in faith, covered with his blood and righteousness, will find out what heaven is like.

Lord, thank you for the heaven you have prepared for us. Comfort us with the glimpse of heaven we find in your Word as we think of those who are gone. And give us hope for ourselves.

Prayer

Oh, sweet and blessed country,
The home of God's elect!
Oh, sweet and blessed country
That eager hearts expect!
Jesus, in mercy bring us
To that dear land of rest;
You are with God the Father
And Spirit ever blest. Amen.

25

An End to Tears

[The Sovereign LORD] will swallow up death forever. The Sovereign LORD will wipe away the tears from all faces.

Isaiah 25:8 (NIV)

Will the tears ever stop? Just when I think I'm out of the woods, something triggers my memory, and I am dabbing tears again. Please, tell me again that this reaction is natural, that the journey through grief not only takes time but is filled with setbacks.

I cry because of my loss, not because of my loved one's gain. For him, death was delivery. It wasn't just his exit from my life, it was his entrance into eternal life with Jesus. Though I cry, let my tears not be tainted with fear but tinted with joy. Let them be dabbed, and even dried completely, by the soft tissues of your sure promises of eternal life. The more I trust those promises, the sooner my tears of loss will evaporate.

You said that you swallowed up death forever. When I swallow something, it's gone. It seems to disappear. It doesn't seem to exist anymore. Remind me that when Jesus swallowed death, it disappeared completely. Though it lurks all around me, though it has claimed my loved one, death really is gone. "Death has been swallowed up in victory" is how Paul put it in his great resurrection chapter (1 Corinthians 15:54). It still growls like some toothless dog, but it can't bite. It still threatens like some mean thug, but its punches can't bruise. Jesus has paid the wage of my sin on Calvary's cross. He has swallowed up death forever. Death is no longer the wage of my sin, it's the escalator to heaven. Because of Jesus, the last beat of my heart becomes the soft knock at heaven's door. When Jesus opens that door, as only he can, I'll be home forever.

Tears still come, off and on, and probably will for some time. But not tears for my loved one. He already knows by experience what Isaiah's words mean, "[The Sovereign Lord] will swallow up death forever." So will I when, by God's grace, I stand with my loved one at the side of the conqueror of death and the giver of life.

Prayer

Lord, I began my journey through grief with tears in my eyes. When those tears linger, please wipe them with the tissue of your promises. Let the sure hope of eternal life for all who die with faith in you be my ongoing comfort and the answer for my tears. Amen.